Joel Deane was born in 1969 and grew up in regional Victoria and Melbourne. He had numerous poems published between 1990 and 1995, but then moved to California and, although he continued writing, fell silent until 2004.

Subterranean Radio Songs, which is Joel's first collection of poetry and won the IP Picks Award for Best Poetry in 2005, tells the story of those silent years.

Joel has worked as a newspaper reporter at The Sun News-Pictorial in Melbourne, a TV and Internet producer in San Francisco, and a press secretary and speechwriter for the Australian Labor Party. He is the author of the IP Picks 2004 winning novel, Another, and is currently speechwriter to the Premier of Victoria, Steve Bracks.

Joel lives in Melbourne with his wife and two children.

The Emerging Authors Series showcases the best new Australian literary talent and is available in digital and print form.

Subterranean Radio Songs

Joel Deane

Brisbane

Interactive Press
an imprint of Interactive Publications
Treetop Studio • 9 Kuhler Court
Carindale, Queensland, Australia 4152
sales@ipoz.biz
www.ipoz.biz/ip/ip.htm

First published by Interactive Press, 2005
© Joel Deane, 2005

All rights reserved. Without limiting the rights under copyright reserved above, no part of this publication may be reproduced, stored in or introduced into a retrieval system, or transmitted, in any form or by any means (electronic, mechanical, photocopying, recording or otherwise), without the prior written permission of the copyright owner and the publisher of this book.

Printed in 14 pt Arial Black on 12 pt Cochin by GOPRINT, Brisbane, Australia.
Made, printed and bound in Australia.

National Library of Australia
Cataloguing-in-Publication data:

Deane, Joel, 1969- .
Subterranean radio songs.

ISBN 1 876819 31 6.

I. Title. (Series: Emerging authors).

A821.4

for the members of my family; living and dead

There is no country.
Only family.

Acknowledgements

Cover image: Joel Deane

Jacket Design: David Reiter

Author images: Camille Deane

Poems in this collection have previously appeared in: *Antipodes, Australian Book Review, Cordite, Divan, Imago, Meanjin, Muse Apprentice Guild, Overland, Salt-lick, Stylus Poetry Journal, Synaptic Graffiti* (CD-ROM), *The Age, The Weekend Australian* and *Zadok Perspectives.*

Thanks to: Sara Moss for her editing of this collection; Dr David Reiter for his ongoing support; Peter Rose for his editorial tweak of 'I build a little house where our hearts once lived'; Kris Hemensley for his sage advice and improving of "Suburban Sonnet"; Paul Mitchell; the late Mal Morgan; Michael Farrell; Sesshu Foster; Michelle T. Clinton; Sophie and Noah Deane; and Kirsten Deane, my first and best critic.

Contents

South

North

South

The bridge at Avenel

The boy has crossed the bridge at Avenel.
Six stone arches stand between us:
Dalrymple's leap over Hughes' piss-weak creek.
The drover's drain that flooded for Red Kelly's sporting son
but did not flow for you.
The boy has crossed the bridge at Avenel.
While you wait on the northern side
find Pat and Ellen.
Forerunners of the economic refugee,
they fled Irish famine to plant themselves
in this cemetery.
The boy has crossed the bridge at Avenel.
I used to think them careless, Pat and Ellen,
for losing so many children.
Martin, the baby they threw overboard
sixty days south of Tipperary, one day shy of Christmas;
the three girls, Margaret, Marianne, Bridget Deane,
who never saw the Board of Works
carve six stone arches from Avenel dirt.
The boy has crossed the bridge at Avenel.
If the creek carried water I could tie
a green cummerbund around my waist,
dive in and try to swim,
join you on the other side,
but the bed is dry, the bridge pushed aside,
I cannot find a way across.
The boy has crossed the bridge at Avenel.
I cannot follow.

The boy sets sail for the past.
Embarks with no letter of introduction.

No vouchsafe from the violence
of the man who would mark his place with a bookmark
of a fist.

No clause containing a kernel of paternal wisdom.
The only knowledge he carries is that which is written
in bones.

Softly, you say, 'Kiss me here.'
I glide back up
until my belly sticks to your belly.

Your lips kiss my lips,
and, as we each map each other,
as we take our place in this
the most tender human duty,

I feel the heat of our ancestors.
Crowding round,
they massage our solitary skin

with naked hands.

My father speaks
a foreign language.
Shadow meanings.
Sawn-off statements.
Same old questions
    about the car.

When I was home
he never hit me.
He never held me.
(He never knew.)

We just drove round.
Never touching.
Always watching
what we said.

My father is a model
discontinued.
One owner only.
Straight, simple lines.
Doors that *Clunk*
    when they close.

Though I mourn, it is not for you:
The grey-flannelled Buddha
who always sat
in the art-deco kitchen
at Castle Deane.

Growling about Bob Santamaria
and Labor thugs.
Drinking cold Carlton Bitter
from a pewter mug.

My father,
the boy you sent down to Melbourne
in a charcoal suit,
told me stories over time
of a lawyer: gruff and regal in his prime.
But my father's voice
I never heard.

I was a child:
You were a statue.

I am a man:
You are a grudge.

The grey-flannelled Buddha
I'll never know.
The first god to ever
wear brown-suede brogues.

The long winter after Eva Fay

Old timers used to tell my old man,
so he told me,
that driving to and from Nagambie —
    ploughing channels for irrigation
    with their skinny, muddy tyres —
they'd pass old Pat —
    son of Michael, da of young Pat,
    pop of Barry, great pa of me —
carrying his pushbike by the frame;
careful not to mark the courtroom suit
he kept crisp by pressing the strides flat
between the mattress and the base

of his single bed.

Mooroopna

Scissor kicking warmed cotton sheets,
and talcum-powdered children sank into hibernation softly.
Sank into the longest evening of the year, nose to nose,
     where no amount of friction would warm their frozen toes.

Waves of murmurs washed beneath the bedroom door crack,
dissolved into the secret summer of three black-footed children,
     four cold months back
—lolling under the timber bridge chewing the fat
—spying teenage bodies uncovered in the razor grass
     off the Goulburn River track
—playing soldier-heads with savage imaginations
—watching the convoy of fruit-picking caravans
     and black legs outside the doors of public lounges
—riding round the shire's yellow lawns
     past triple-front brick-veneer houses.

Back when only the occasional adult word pushed into the shade.
Into our world of pool day and fete day
     and the ANZAC Day parade.

When I was a child my mother's kitchen table was forever paved
with the margarine-smeared bellies of white and brown bread
   slices.
Come lunchtime, the cannery's production line crammed into our
   milkbar.
The one in McLennan Street across the road from the water
   tower
where I raced my brother Tim—two-hundred laps flat out—
then fell—flat out—on my back in the cool grass
            as the sky reeled above me.

Inside our double-fronted shop,
where the stock was piled to the ceiling
and you needed a stepladder to reach the beans and baby potatoes,
the fruit pickers badgered Dad to cash a cheque, give some credit
or sauce a Four'n'Twenty pie—while Tim, my sister Liza and I
            played behind the long counter.

The kitchen was out back, through the swinging door.
It was there Mum spent those summer days.
Patrolling the rows of bread slices—blurred hands doling out
tomato, ham and beetroot, pineapple, lettuce,
chicken-loaf and cheese with practiced ease.
            Forever making other people's lunches.

I am standing on a chair at the sink, shelling boiled eggs.
Heat radiates from solid-yellow hearts, scalding fingertips.
Shells splinter as I peel, catching beneath fingernails.
I am day-dreaming about winning Tattslotto.
Taking Mum away on one of those ocean-liners—

the kind with sundecks and shuffleboards,
peanut-shaped pools and exotic destinations.
        A place where Mum could sit down for lunch.

I drop my first shelled egg
into the plastic bowl filled with cold water.
It hits the bottom
—splashes the lino—
reminds me of my favourite Commando comic:
The one about patrol boats
where the sailors plug soap into the depth-charge fuse
        to make it sink deeper.

'Finished yet?' Mum asks.
'Not yet. Nearly,' I say—
picturing the soap dissolve
as the depth charge descends.
By the time I finish shelling the customers are waiting.
        They all want sandwiches today.

Mum starts mashing the eggs.
One has a red ribbon through its centre,
but Mum doesn't notice.
She sloshes in more Midlands Milk,
mashes again, and, before long, the ribbon is gone—
        mixed in with everything else.

Tell me again, as the moon rises.

About that time at Rosebud
when you lost yourself, then were found;
and how Grandma B sewed on your bathers
Property of campsite 53.

How you performed at Gordon Street,
cartwheeling on the front lawn
while everyone sat on the verandah — clapping you
and fanning themselves with the *Sporting Globe.*

About those long January afternoons
at the Coburg baths with Boompa;
wet hair slicked back like a Cuban,
evaporating on the buckled concrete.

As the moon rises, tell me again.

It takes timing to catch
at the crossing
the Dookie train
without stopping:
engine gunning a tick
          over sixty kays;
chassis straining
to meet — broadside —
the barrelling blunt end
of the weekly freighter
          — unforgiving,
incapable of stopping —
that clips the toenails
of bald hills licked dry
by northerlies,
bronzing the world
with a red chalk frosting
that bloods the brash of metal
where the freighter caught

the car.

1. *Divertimento*

Viewing the body
in an open casket
of a blue plastic dish
on the linen fold
of a surgical mask —
as the unexpectant mother
          is wheeled away to theatre —
the newborns of St Vincent's
serenade our stillborn

with their cries.

2. Residua

Break the cot back down to its prefabricated state.
Bag it in black plastic bags.
Stack it behind the bookshelves in the double garage.
Call the people who need to know.
Let them know.

Let all incoming calls go to voicemail.
Eat takeaway.
Don't do the dishes.
Watch TV. Forget to watch (or return) a DVD.

Lie in bed.
Circumnavigate the house.
Lie on the kitchen floor.

Park at Timber Ridge.
Watch nameless neighbours walk laps of the football oval.
Listen to the last of a Good Friday that cannot speak a single
   word.

3. Postmortem

i.

'There is a bruise in the small of my back
from where the needle burned.
I could not feel when they reached inside to pull outside
      the last pieces of our baby.'

ii.

      'Words are landfill
bulldozed into place to fill an empty landscape
      that yawns beneath a cloud
of pestilent gulls.'

iii.

'I am still bleeding.
Yet to regain feeling.'

iv.

      'We build barricades of words
for our protection.'

v.

'I blame myself for the shadow heart
that stopped
beating.'

vi.

      'No words,
no one thing, could keep the child from being born

to silence.'

4. In Utero

The womb of the incinerator
now holds you

at nine-hundred degrees
centigrade.

Conversation on the midnight stream

   'Are you sleeping?'
'I want to,
I've been trying to,
but I cannot
sleep.'
   'Don't worry.
Time's black tide will catch us soon,
then we'll both be sleeping.'

'A welcome sleep?'
   'A welcome knowledge.'
'I'd rather a welcome memory —

Like Ubud.'

   'Watching you swim through darkness
until you surfaced, and the fairy lights
showed your true colour.'

'Lying awake in rooms without walls,
other than humidity,
while white flags floated on the current of a lazy breeze
like ghosts along the rice terraces —
such memories are a comfort that oils the heart.
Like my last summer in Sydney:
That January was a string of perfect days.'

   'With who?'
'Someone you never knew.

One day we caught the train in from Parramatta
and picnicked on Observatory Hill, above the Harbour.
We sat in the sun and drank warm champagne,
laughing at the view.

The sky and water were flawless shades of blue.'

     'Then my memories are perfect, too,
because I recall everything about you.
What you wore the first day we met.
What you said over sushi at Kuni's.
My head is crammed with shiny objects.'

'Then tell me a perfect time.'

In the distance,
traffic on the freeway passes with a sigh.

     'Late morning at Echuca Road:
The house with a paddock for a backyard
and a cool hollow for a front lawn.

Overhead, clouds perform circus tricks
as my great-grandfather holds me high.
I'm not yet two-years-old
and his ancient hands are rough on my baby skin;
but his face is warm
     and as big as the sun.'

I build a little house
where our hearts once lived

A master bedroom, a stripped mattress
dead centre of the floor.
Plastic dishes in the kitchen sink,
soft toys kicked against the wall.
Ikea furniture flat in boxes,
I assemble you without a key;
no need for Swedish instruction,
these hands know your symmetry.
Finished with bedevilled edges,
hewn from raw blonde pine,
inner suburban by desire,
Scandinavian by design.

I build a little house where our hearts
once lived—remake rooms I cannot find.

Suburban sonnet

The fool walks in darkness.
Finds the long way home.
Navigates via satellite
& SMSes on a mobile phone.

Children all soundly sleeping.
Wife alone in bed.
Backyard dogs herald the fool,
bark out names of the dead.

There is no dinner waiting.
No conjugal embrace.
Such comforts were abandoned
in a dark, suburban place.

And, as he passes a wizened tree,
the fool realizes where he left his key.

1.

The freckled boy is now a man —

Open-eyed dreaming, he sits as his tram traces the metallic spine
of a north-eastern suburban line.
A brick wall, twelve feet tall, races the tram down a hill,
     glowering,
blood orange in the flush of the evening sun.
Mesmerized, he would not notice if, in the cemetery beyond the wall,
the Stone Virgin broke moorings. Led north
a squadron of Granite Angels,
     In formation, they climb and wheel away,
     shuddering Norfolk pines
     with the tips of heavy, heavy wings.

The tram overtakes the wall, rails into a gully
as the freckled man slips into the arms
of a freckled boy not yet nine.

2.

There,
the sun is high; so, too, the river.
A sandbank cushions an elbow of the Goulburn
where the boy dives,
     arms extended,
from a platform tree, causing surface ripples
as he searches for snags with chewed fingernails.

He has been told not to swim here.
He knows that,
     down deep, deep down,
the holes harbour Murray Cod.

He remembers how, last summer,
when the river level fell,
they found tissue paper,
   once the muscle of a man,
stretched over sunken branches.
He has spied the old man in the humpy
downstream.
   Lives off carp's hearts! boys say.
   Eats them alive! boys cry.
And he has smelt McLennan Street
in fruit-picking season; stained with ripe fruit,
blood and sunburned fornication.
But this summer the water is deep.
And even fear cannot stand the heat.

The sun is high.

The air is dry.

And the freckled boy is alone.

3.

Arms extending
     Legs frog-kicking
         Lungs exploding
Mind expanding
at the thought he is nearing the end of his first decade,
the boy's skin shivers as he dives—his scrotum shrinks.

He feels himself dissolve
as he dives deep into a dream,
   arms pinned to sides,
where he finds himself double-kicking
beside a tram.

And in the window sits a man.

Stealing into Portsea.
Digging deep into the sand with plastic spades beneath the shadow
of the shed
of Lindsay Fox,
I heard a sound—and turned in time to see Port Phillip swallow
my children.

Ankle-biters are amphibious.
Barge, blue-arsed—squealing—
through the ankle-rollers.
Seek the setting sun.

The beach is broad enough
to break a ship upon.
A steel coffin caught
     —flat—
against the horizon.
Carrying at three-quarter
capacity to clear
     the heads.

Taking a stick
I trace the
besotted path, the
haphazard circum-
ambulation that
ends at this
holiday des-
tination.
     A cross-hatched concentric circuit around a nubbin
of compacted sand.

Driving without headlights
I can see
what's oncoming.

What's oncoming
I can see
driving without headlights.

Driving without headlights
what's oncoming
I can see.

I can see
driving without headlights
what's oncoming.

What's oncoming
driving without headlights
I can see.

I can see
what's oncoming
driving without headlights.

(What's oncoming
cannot see
me.)

Arriving in darkness
—enclosed by mountains backlit
   by a low full moon—
we slept but did not soar.
Felt the mountains in our dreams.

Awoken next morning
—seeing the sheet of stone walls
   and trees—
we saw ourselves.
The fear of blind flight.

Aware of our gravity
—a sinker tied with fishing line tight
   around the heart—
we spoke over breakfast of heavy sleep.
Too much lead for feeble wings.

Afterwards, after climbing
—our feet counting the granite ceiling's
   granite spine—
we stood at the pinnacle, thought of falling.
To know a sky's true colour.

Boy in landscape

for Noah

Rubber-soled shoes tattoo the veranda.
Fists of furious delight pound unmade garden beds.
Piff pink/purple/red balls of varying circumference —
       sound after them at a clip-clop.
Enchant Tranter: *Dog paddle! Back pedal!*
Inveigle a quadrangle of eggshell blue
to dwell down upon these courtyard games.
       A perpetual blur in the periphery of frame.

The secrets of happy children cannot be decrypted.
    Reverse engineered, road tested
    on rodents; rubber stamped
    in Rockville.
Patented and air-freighted
in child-proof containers to our faux-republic
in the Pacific
at a premium

when it is generic brands we prefer.

Imperial Chemicals

1.

Since when could the enamel of an ancient incisor trace an artifact
back
to the foothills
of Stone Age Wales?

Everything, it seems, even history,
can be reduced
to chemistry.

2.

A pair of superannuated fossils of Imperial Chemicals
stand in faded golf apparel
to measure the acidity of a swimming pool of shiraz.

A remaindered crop once planted in the superphosphorous
of tax
deductibility.

As the lights slowly roll green to red and back again
we wait in the outside lane for our turn
and when it comes I gun it to the floor
Through first second   third fourth   then overdrive
with the landscape towering and throbbing through
my one-way mind at the speed of
                              but watch me now
double-clutch then handbrake slide into Lorimer Street
with the chassis squealing in expectation of
                              Never mind
Now we're passing customs houses and steel ships and
nothing lives in Port Melbourne but work-time
and quit-time and pubs with early morning licenses
Nothing   But it doesn't matter when my wheel turns
and the tyres answer   Nothing matters but
a cigarette to suck an empty road   And speed
without a Jack in sight   Or a wharfie strike ·
Which reminds me as I hoon a killer roundabout
outside the GMH plant at Fisherman's Bend
                              and side-step
the speed trap
              in a four-wheel drift
and half expect
              to see Pine Gap looming in my rear-view
mirror (it's so much like the moon out here)   Then
my speedo begins to shake   And I touch the photo of you
sticky-taped to the dashboard in a sort-of-tender moment
And I can feel my skull contracting   Crushing
those thoughts   so I wait for it to rupture
                              and punch

the brake or accelerator (it doesn't matter
which)
      Nothing matters
Not when I'm in this abandoned State   Driving under Westgate
Slashing our headlights across the cold factory faces
sitting between the scrub weeds that grow
in the most desolate places   Our lights run like a laser stick
They run
        Factory   Weeds   Truck depot   Weeds
Craters piled with crap   Weeds   Coode Island   Weeds
Chemical plants flushing out their smoke-stacks   Weeds
Smouldering mercury clouds   Weeds   (Waiting
for something to break)   Weeds   (For a meteorite
to strike)   Weeds
                Weeds
                    Weeds
                        And I need control
since I just missed a bruiser of a power pole
But keep rattling on anyway   Around   Under Westgate
Without a glance at the speedo or a word of the insides
that died when their outsides became
                    Too strong
                    Too fast
for everything to hold together
The overhead traffic crossing the Yarra just a stone's throw
from the BP refinery is Spartan   This is a New World
of real estate for those buttoned-down
                  Jeez
that was a tight sweeper And my engine is overdubbing
every thought I squeeze between gear changes
                      Brake
Accelerate now   Gas it hard   Let the tyres
bite
      She shudders   I can't allow the noise to die now

because then I'll be listening to the blood pumping
through my head   Even louder   Even faster
So follow the strip around the waterfront toward St Kilda
with the sea air funnelling through the unravelled
window   Slow a little to pass under Westgate   Make sure
everything's buckled in

                              Sometimes I stop here
(but   you know   I can't   always stay)   And always
is never just that   Never certain   Once I did stop but
And I watched the tide and the navigator's pylons
mar each belt of breakers

                              Slicing them into easy pieces
                              to pound the subdivided beachfront
I watched until the engine
cut out

          And the terrible nothing started up   Crowding me
you know   Choking me with the loss of something   Waiting
on an answer even when there's nothing to say (Nothing much)

North

America bleeds
    across the horizon —

wears Radial Steel
    tyres down,

burns bare arms
    and faces brown,

smells of unleaded
    Techron gasoline,

beats bugs against our
    fissured windscreen,

lies in the blur
    of southern grass,

watches, silent,
    as we pass.

Seeking solace
in the song,
a melody for rhyming days,
I take the T
from Wellington.
     Crossing the River Mystic,
a yard I pass
—muddy sod of shag-pile grass—
where Medford's suburban fleet
has run aground, fibreglass hulls
all scrubbed down.
     All winter long
the boats stood on stilts
watched the Mystic whisper past;
Now, come cold spring,
they hear my train sing on:
You are your father;
     You are your son.
A karaoke that echoes
the cadence of
your naked ways;
A song heard
ever since the embarcadero
     of our days.

Staying at the Waldorf.
Sleeping in the Cole Porter suite.
      As good a place as any for our Jazz Age to end.

It was September, our first time in the City,
and we were living beyond our means;
catching Joni Mitchell taxis from New York cliché to cliché,
      taking all the right pictures.

I had packed a duffel bag of my best Californian clothes;
You, as ever, an immaculate selection of earthy hues,
      and enough Estée Lauder to hide your heroin eyes.

Still, you can never out-dress a New Yorker.
Walking Fifth Avenue I was struck by the collective sound
      of those expensive shoes;

Tiptoed back to the Waldorf in my Polish brogues
where, while you locked yourself in the bathroom,
      I began to roam barefoot —

Scrunch my toes in all that five-star carpet,
play Chop Sticks on Porter's baby grand, prowl
      for the perfect souvenir.

Summer storm, Las Vegas

I ride into town on the back of a summer storm that closes roads,
floods five-thousand room hotels,
swells the desert so much so that it reclaims streets,
hovers on the Red Rock horizon, threatens to swallow the city,
leave New York New York's Lady Liberty shattered,
abandoned like Shelley's trunkless Ozymandias
      —disturbs the neon din of casino commerce for a while.

I book into the Flamingo Hilton before midnight,
am three hundred down by four;
my better judgment awash in a cocktail tide
      of martinis and margaritas.

I should know better.
This is my fifth time in Las Vegas,
and the afterglow of that first Vegas win
      has long since begun to sting.

I finish my margarita.
Walk outside.
Remember how to sweat.
Request that the room service enclose and air-condition
the Boulevard upon my return.
Wade into the night,
behind the town's casino facade,
past empty sand lots, overflown strip joints, fresh storm drains;
deep into the cul-de-sacs of a company town—
wash up in the castaway courtyard of the Nevada Suites,
where lucky losers rent apartments
      week-to-week.

The courtyard is quiet.
I kick my legs over the crater of a peanut-shaped pool.
Sit, evaporating in the humidity.
Watch the naked light bulb inside number four on the second floor
simmer its sealed room to the boil.

I watch until the door opens, flooding the courtyard
with molten yellow light, and a working girl exits:
The cleft of her bare cheeks winking
below the cuff of her gold lamé dress.

She tells me later she is not American.
And I tell her I am not surprised.
Because, when she stood beside me, above me,
pumps teasing the precipice
        of the concrete pool,
I found covetous her crooked smile.

(Flying over California.)

The mountains

    The desert

        Wore the late afternoon

like soft sand suede.

Berkeley, California

Hard-baked.
Blanketed with gum trees.
Each evening
the houses embedded
in your hills
begin to blaze.
Windows of their eyes
blinded
from staring into

the sun.

43

Seven feet south of where it should be,
the sedan's far nose strays into another lane.
A horn.
     A swerve.
And, once again, I am where I should be.
Driving the I-80.
Finding my way, carefully,
in a hired car. Fumbling with the radio
because the tape-deck won't play.

Nothing is where it should be —
Traffic coming on from my left, not my right,
People turning, never stopping, at red lights,
Glove-boxes holding .38s instead of flashlights.
And I am thinking: So *this* is America.
     Land of opportunity.
     Pizza crusts stuffed with pepperoni.

I pay a dollar to ride the Bay Bridge into San Francisco,
conjuring images of a younger, thinner Michael Douglas
—steely eyed—
standing beside Karl Malden.
And eternal car-chases, up
               and down
these whiplash streets.

A dollar does not afford a view,
just a peek of the Golden Gate's orange towers
peeking through a glacier of fog.
I check the mirror.

I check the speedo.
Try to indicate, but on flick the wipers.
Change lanes anyway.
        Turn up the radio.

I am waiting for a song.
Something heavy, yet melodic.
A number from my internal soundtrack
—Down By the River, Cortez the Killer
        or Cowgirl in the Sand—
As I slow, then steady;
take the tunnel
        into Treasure Island.

You never do what you're told.
Buying that hot-pink raincoat with the big zipper down the front
and the Little Heidi-hood when I said it looked bloody stupid.

And now you've gone out in it, saying you want cars to see you
crossing the road.
And now a tremor hits
                    —a tectonic speedhump
                    beneath my desk.

And I think of you riding that one out.
Prepared for the rain, but nothing else.

They brace the building with steel
—lucky wings snapped from the Bay Bridge—
spray down the brick warehouse walls
with an anti-earthquake (placebo) spray.
Claim we could survive a *Loma Prieta* replay,
but exit before the pile drivers start to pound
and the steel supports begin to hum and torque
like King Kong's goddamn tuning fork.

Luger pistol

for William S. Burroughs

We play William Tell.
What better way to mark Burroughs' passing
from Beat to truly beat, we decide over Tequila,
salt crystals and diamond-hard methamphetamines.

But we have no apple. No fruit of any tree.
Just stale pizza, a crate of empty vodka bottles;
a luger pistol brought back to Montana from Omaha;
passed down from Butte to Berkeley to here—
        a dead soldier's souvenir.

Zorca takes the war trophy;
cleans and oils, snaps the firing pin into place;
comes back from the kitchen saying
a Mexican candle beats a Swiss apple any day.

So we cut straws.
Agree that long stands, short shoots.
Draw destiny from Zorca's fist:
Which finds you against the firing wall,
balancing a Lent candle above your Magdalene face;
Which finds me weighing the luger pistol in my hand,
knowing how heavy is your heart as I try to stand
sober—

I cannot shoot straight sitting down.

At last alone,
they pound through mercury waters to the west.

No aphrodisiac can be creamed from their bones.
No aperitif carved from such ancient flesh.

Once, they were desired.

Fatigue-green eyes.
Shell-shock dreams.
Purple-heart breast.

Khaki girl,
no camouflage
can hide the fact:

You are at war.

The procedure was a success, you say afterward.
Lying in your floral gown and matching shower cap;
waiting in Grand Central Station, the HMO* ward,
      to be taken home.

You smile your mother's smile. Hold your baby hands out
for me to hold. Tell how it felt when they excavated your breast,
flung their picks and shovels on your bare belly, tunnelled for
      the malignant seam.

HMOs, or Health Maintenance Organisations, are the major form of health insurance
in the United States.

1.

You never lose
your baggage.

It travels
an alternate route

from Berkeley
to Katmandu

until the Sherpas
find you.

2.

Hands soaked
in iodine.

Face numb
to sunshine.

Air too anxious
to inhale.

You trek the Himalayan trail.

Intoxicated
by carbon-dioxide.

Boots blistering
on the inside.

Monitoring any change
in mood.

You are climbing at altitude.

3.

Peter wrote from Pokhara.

Said the Annapurna Range
was buried

beneath a prescription haze
two days deep.

Your heart burns
white
the greyscale screen,
melts
the electromagnetic
snow.

I splice the silent
video
to my master
reel.
(What colour do you
feel?)

If I really am
the caregiver

you must be
the caretaker

I suppose.

Our longing,

a naked body left
lonely in the dark,

broods over us
in our dreams,

rubs against us
in the shower,

stares us down
without speaking

—outlives us all.

If I still held
my ruby rosary beads
        in the pocket
of the winter coat
        not worn for years
and could recall
        the *glory be* that came
after thumbing through
        the joyful—
the sorrowful—
        the glorious—
the luminous
        mysteries
I'd pray that prayer,
        Hail—my oh my—
hail my unholy queen,
        (turn to steam).

Sir Francis Drake slept here.
They are just visiting—
measuring the weathered beach,
stride for stride—as,
to the left, cliffs of lemon sandstone slide,
to the right, slate waves pave the shore.

They drove west from Berkeley. Crossed
Richmond Bridge, took Sir Francis Drake Boulevard,
wound their way to Point Reyes Station;
seeking a location to match their abstract mood.
Protagonists in a foreign film shot according to
the Danish school. A stone in Lars von Trier's shoe.

He crushes a coffee cup of polystyrene
in his bare hand.
She walks beside,
a shifting center of gravity;
the catalyst of each and every scene.

The beach is longer than it seems.
Crowded
with body bags of seaweed, timber sleepers,
and dancing black crows.
If he were a method actor
he might chase those pirate birds into the watchful sky,
then stand alone,
knee-deep in the Pacific foam,
while she, loath to steal his scene,
stayed behind, remained in frame,
wringing hands that are never clean.

But, being more Merchant Ivory
than Martin Scorsese,
they stand silent on the shore.

Wait for the crows to wheel away.

Then, wordlessly, agree;
it is time to turn back again.

Lying, legless,
amidst the wreckage
of the livingroom,

While you sleep
with the dirty dishes
in the bedroom,

The washbasin
whines
from the bathroom —

begs I open
the window,

fall six storeys

to the street.

Once upon a time,
when the world was waiting—
        a concubine reclining upon a couch,
crisp as cranberry juice and frozen vodka;
a panorama of a basement view
        that took me by surprise—
I was overwhelmed by the comfort
promise can bring.
        Wished upon a star for foolish things.

I excavate the sorrow.
Plumb the depth of her days.
Mine the stratigraphy of marrow
for metal of the Mesozoic age.

Here hammered the god-botherers—
brass din of bold, of brave—
who claimed me as a lifesaver
when I saw her in a swaddled grave:

My America, my first daughter
who, tenfold times, tried to be born
might yet resurrect the father
from the strata that has formed.

Trisomy 21

for Sophie

Our grief is largely guilt
for the things—thoughts, words, actions
formerly catachised as *sins*—
which cannot be exorcised
without abandoning euphemism
for its more belligerent cousin.
Truth be told, there is a statistic
that does not lie, a doctor who will
categorically state *we all must die*,
a geneticist who does not see herself
as the goddess of the summer solstice
that is the daisy chain of evolution;
an uncommon cloud of pollen that is a child.
And she is lovely. And she is dear to me.

The house was a room short,

we thought.
Spoke *ad nauseam* of alteration:
Renovation of the double garage,
a nursery in our corner yard.
But the house has our measure,
it seems.

Pack away the plans
and maternity jeans.

1.

I can barely
see
Port Phillip Bay
     (a vulva of
     blue-grey)
from our
St Vincent's Private
suite.

2.

Eyes smoking
from the potbelly of brown coal
I am stoking

I step out
into a pizzling
that has turned to steam:

tastes like kerosene.

You are not the woman I desired; and I,
I am not the man you desired me to be:
He lies on the lilo before a big-screen TV,
subsiding slowly, cerebrum toasted by
static electricity (a suburban lobotomy).
Just as our mallei cannot choose the sounds
they sing, it comes to pass, inevitably,
that the involuntary muscle of the heart pounds
out the cynical tom-tom of discovery
of the sordid self made by circumstance;
when youth's tattoo triggers a naked line dance
against the jolly polka of middle-aged ubiquity.

I keep channel surfing, but at every change see
a chorus line of dancers; each identical to me.

While we are apart I will
wear no shoes, walk barefoot
over Nevada sands, tune my heart
to 33 kilohertz, synchronize
my inner ear to terra firma, and,
using Nikola Tesla's method,
send my speechless self tunnelling
beneath Death Valley and the Sierra
—via the subterranean radio—
so that I might reach you
driving in San Francisco,
broadcast my white noise
through your car stereo
(and blow out all
        your speakers).

1.

The day was silver,
turned to rust.
>Not yet five, but almost dusk.

2.

Black dog pisses
on damp dead leaves.
>Sheets of birds rise over naked trees.

3.

Shadow covers an Empire
sun does not shine upon.
>The black, black dog is on the run.

Driving without chains,
we raced through the north country
as a marble sky threatened to break across
      our bare heads.

Come Glasgow
we let the Volkswagen turn into an igloo of German engineering.
Walked the pink-stone streets.
Ate Chinese food deep fried.
Spoke of the woodwork of Charles Rennie Mackintosh.
Watched a double-decker bus three-step down a street
      in a slow circling waltz.

Our restlessness becalmed
by recurring visions of the burning car that,
driving north on the motorway, loomed

out of zero visibility.

Molten waves boil over
black basalt coagulations.
Spelling stones, Pelé's
bleach-white bones,
litter the volcanic shore.
In remembrance, they say;
     Forever yours.

I leave no message.
For these bones
are not ready to be written.
And the sea, a pupil
darker than an inkwell
of India-blue,
     cannot read.

Gaudalupe

They call my bus the Marco Polo, but it is going nowhere.
Stranded, ninety miles north of Mexico City;
surrounded by the liberated sierras of Subcommandante Marcos.
    A feathered serpent of tail lights snaking in the darkness.

So, *buenas noches*, my love.
Forgive me, *por favor*; do not forget me.

I am waiting upon Our Lady of Gaudalupe.
A glorietta in balaclava—toting a guerilla's bouquet—
she blockades the highway
while I, some kind of pilgrim,
    cannot find the words to pray.

1.

To fish
in this post-Soviet bloc, present-*Americano* blockade
of a Special Period
in the twilight of a Habana Vieja teeming
with *Habaneros* toting handlines
is no leisure activity.
It is economic necessity.

I swim a near dark as close as communal bath water.
Dodge the lines of *jiniterismo* visible by the whites
of their smiles.
(*No, novia. Gracias*, I say;
I don't want to be your pony.)

Moskovitchs grind, bicycles glide
past — accompany a cluster of musicians
wheezing Buena Vista Social Club tunes
to tempt the tourists.
(*Lo siento, amigo*, I shrug smile;
I don't wish to salsa your *hermana*.)

A crowd gathers.
Police down arms to hammer a human horseshoe
around a whippet of a man, body bowed
like one of those graphite poles sportsmen wield
in the Gulf Stream. Drinking *mojitos*,
thinking themselves Ernest.

The crowd contracts,
confirms that Communism is a centipede.

Once-upon-a-time comrades
compressed
into a collective, many-legged desire
for consumer goods—computers, cellulars,
wide-screen TVs, air conditioners, flash cars,
fresh food.

2.

Before my arrival
my Mexican *familiaris* intimated all Castro had to offer
was contraband tobacco
and Cuban fellatio.
More question than information, as I recall.
But I contended I desired only baseball.

Saw myself behind the batter's cage
at Estadio Latinamericano
sipping espresso from a paper thimble,
listening to the bleacher calls.

The eternal search for the elusive
curve ball.

3.

Strike two. Ball three.

The count is full.
The crowd aroused.
The pitch waist high
and hard—

Begging to be hit.

4.

I came to Cuba carting a cardboard suitcase
and a straw hat.

I am highly flammable,
         but buy a carton of *Romeo y Julieta*.
My passport has expired,
         but I possess greenbacks.
I think myself alone,
         but have a suede-headed chaperone:

My kid sister.

Together, we have ridden the Yucatan
in second-class bus carriages.
Both of us in remission
from births, deaths
and marriages.

Habana Vieja is our last stop in the Americas.
South of Cuba is suburbia —
mortgages, marriage to my West Indies,
a long suffering Baptist bride,
and children I am yet to name.
Call them Nina, Pinta, Santa Maria.
Call me Columbus. Better yet, Cortez.

5.

The promise of capitalism thrashes about
in Bahia de la Habana,
fights for freedom,
threatens to baptise the fisherman.
But the fish cannot outlast the centipede.

As each fisherman is bent to breaking
he is relieved by fresh hands
until, rotation by rotation,
the prize is reeled in
                —gaffed, netted—
left to drown
on the warm concrete
in the late evening
of Castro's Cuba.

A panting
yellow-fin tuna
with a torso as thick
as a man's thigh.

I've been meaning to write
since the suicide bomber
in Tel Aviv.

Another blind delivery boy of fate
lost to the tide of blood history.

Dragged back and forth by the gravity
of an indifferent moon.

Walking the white sands
beside warm water the colour
of Listerine,
          despite the heat
the soles of bare feet
don't burn

Because the white sand
is not white sand
          —not really—
but the desiccated, denuded bones
of *gringos* who have gone
blithely barefoot before.

Playing roulette
on the slow boat to Bermuda,
the circumambulated roll
of the Norwegian Princess
keeps the silver ball from finding
lucky twenty-four.
　　　　But I keep punting.
On deck, leeward side,
New Jersey snowbirds rotate
on banana-lounge rotisseries
as, astern, on the horizon,
America melts away:
Soft bodies barbecued slow,
like Corky's prime pork pulled
　　　　tender from the bone.
Below, in the casino,
a TV dinner ballroom walled
with silver foil, the craps crowd
overacts, hoots every winning roll,
while my cockney croupier spins the wheel
so hard the Princess turns to starboard.
And the silver ball finds five
for the fifth time.
　　　　So much for long division.

Peas & gravy

With thanks to Michael Farrell's 'what are ys'

I eat roast beef with fingers
while Dr Vicky prepares my wife.

I join the dots of Michael Farrell:
pick at this peas & gravy life.

Presented with a pair of plastic forks
I am told my need for control will lessen

as my ear grows. But how, tell me now,
can I carve a roast with those?

I was told—
and this is no urban mythology—
that, together with his brain tumor, surgeons
cut away this man's memory.
Pruned him back to seventeen.

Perhaps that is what happened here.

I leave America,
Land of makeovers, seeking something more
      than motion.
I leave America.
My doodle-dandy daughter my only Yankee
      souvenir.
I leave America.
Ship myself south in pieces; bubble-wrapped
      and boxed, bound for Port Melbourne.

But never quite arrive.